The Hawk

Keystone's

The Hawk

An Improvisational Play
by
Murray Mednick
and
Tony Barsha

Photographs by Ralph Gibson
Designed by Quentin Fiore

The Bobbs-Merrill Company, Inc.
Indianapolis and New York

The Bobbs-Merrill Company, Inc.
A Subsidiary of Howard W. Sams & Co., Inc., Publishers
Indianapolis • Kansas City • New York

THE HAWK was first produced at Theatre Genesis, St. Mark's Church in-the-Bowery, on Friday, October 13, 1967. The cast was as follows:

The Chinese Opium Smoker Ching Yeh
The Hawk Tony Serchio
The Double Lee Kissman
The First Victim Sally Sommer
The Second Victim O-Lan Johnson
The Inspector Walter Hadler
The Third Victim Scarlett Johnson
The Fourth Victim Barbara Young
The Dealer Walter Hadler

THE HAWK was subsequently produced by James Walsh and Dina and Alexander E. Racolin at The Actor's Playhouse on April 17, 1968 with the same cast. Both productions were directed by Tony Barsha. Music was composed by Eddie Hicks.

Introduction

The Hawk is not like other plays. In its very genesis it represents a radical break with the tradition of Western drama, which from earliest times has been primarily a literary form; first someone wrote the play, and then it was realized by actors. *The Hawk* happened the other way around: it was brought into being by the actors and only subsequently written down. It is primarily a theatrical object, in short, and gains its literary existence after the fact, with its publication in this book.

Let me be more specific. *The Hawk* began with an impressionistic scenario (less than two pages, I think) by Murray Mednick. Then Mednick, a playwright, Tony Barsha, a director, Eddie Hicks, a musician, and nine actors spent two months in the summer of 1967 at the Keystone Dairy Farm in the Pocono Mountains of Pennsylvania, and together they made the scenario into the play. Its authorship is credited to Mednick and Barsha, but in fact most of the lines were improvised by the actors. The characters, their relationships, the events and very words of the play were formed by and of the people who were to play it. Mednick as writer focused on the language, Barsha as director on the staging, and together, in 24-hour-a-day interaction with the players, they found and refined the emerging formal scheme and structure. For all its initial freedom, the work was exactly disciplined. By the time it reached performance, *The Hawk* was almost entirely set, with only a few openings left for improvisation.

This play is one of the first published examples of a widespread and dynamic new impulse in the vanguard theatre of this country. The technique of improvisation is only part of it. Improvisational theatre had its latest vogue in the early 1960's, when the Second City players came from Chicago to Broadway and then settled down Off-Broadway, where *The Premise* had already run through several editions. Despite the brilliance of individual performers, both were limited in ambition, doing tricks and playing games within the revue form. Eventually the possibilities wore thin and the revue improvisers faded away.

Now improvisation is reappearing in a new context, as part of an effort toward genuinely communal theatre work. Necessity mothered a breakthrough when the Living Theatre, exiled in Europe, found itself living for the first time as a coherent community of artists and began to derive the work from that experience of community. Their first group product was *Mysteries and Smaller Pieces,* an anthology of exercises and experiments, made in Paris in 1964. The giant step was *Frankenstein,* premiered in Venice in 1965, which was developed from scratch by the entire Living Theatre company, with Judith Malina acting as director and Julian Beck making key choices of design and scenario. *Frankenstein* is a monumental achievement, its consequences incalculable. The Living Theatre went on to de Brecht's *Antigone* without a director, the staging created by the community; and their new work, *Paradise Now,* is communal all the way.

The new impulse is affecting others. The Open Theatre, directed by Joseph Chaikin, has made a new full-evening work, *The Serpent,* deriving its text from the Bible, and conceived not as a drama but as an ensemble performance piece. The Performance Group, formed by Richard Schechner in a garage in lower Manhattan, did an "environmental" production called *Dionysus in 69,* based on Euripides' *The Bacchae* but developing its staging and much of its text in group workshops exploring interactions among the individual performers. And other such enterprises are appearing fast.

The Hawk will stand as a pioneering use of the communal/improvisational concept to create a thematically and formally coherent fictional drama; and its concise ritualistic structure is a step forward on yet another common front. For, in addition to its peculiar and significant methodology, *The Hawk* is a fine play and functions as well in the ordinary terms: the characters are exotic but sympathetic, their predicaments absorbing, the action provocative in its ambiguity, the lines sharply witty and revealing. Seeing the play in performance was a brilliantly entertaining and deeply exciting experience, at the very least a major event of its season.

To those considering *The Hawk* for production, I would suggest bearing its particular nature in mind. The implication of the method is humanist: the play is for the actors. There's no reason not to cast and produce *The Hawk* like any other play—and good reason to do so. But another possibility might be more interesting: you might take only the frame as given and reopen the seven improvisations, regarding the printed versions only as examples, not casting to type but reimprovising according to your own cast and your own life-style. That would be how to make *The Hawk* your own play and bring life to your stage like maybe never before. *The Hawk* isn't about dope or hipsters or hawks, after all, it's about people.

Michael Smith
Sundance
June 21, 1968

The Hawk

Characters:

THE HAWK
THE DOUBLE
THE FOUR VICTIMS
THE INSPECTOR/DEALER
and
A CHINESE OPIUM SMOKER

Scene:

The stage is bare except for three chairs, center stage, facing the audience, and a single chair, different from the others, placed at an angle, stage left. No props are used.

Prologue

THE CHINESE OPIUM SMOKER enters in the traditional Chinese opium smoker's robe. He goes to downstage center, holds, then begins a sound and movement representation of fire. He builds this to a peak, shouts: "FIRE!", then moves to stage left and addresses the audience:

Fire is reality. It starts with a tiny spark and moves through spontaneous combustion from one layer to another. And the color of fire changes from red, to orange, to yellow, and, as the temperature rises, it changes to blue—yes, blue—and from blue the fire rushes to white heat. Fire then ceases to be real. Fire is but the extension of the object which is burning.

He returns to center stage.

I am the extension of the object which is burning! I am the Almighty Fire God! The Powerful Fire God! The Divine Fire God! Ra, ra, ra! Yes! I am the Powerful Fire God! Ra, ra, ra! Get the fuck out of here, you Water God! You get the fuck out of here! Ra, ra, ra! Let me tell you the story of these ra, ra, ra birds that came to the window of my palace. They want to get high. They want to be divine. Then one day along comes this ra, ra, ra hawk! This ra, ra, ra ridiculous hawk! And he stole the fire from me and gave it to the birds! And the birds all get high, and they all get hot, and they all get burn up. Ra, ra, ra. Don't play with me! If you play with me, you play with fire. I am the Fire God. I am the Divine Fire God. Ra, ra, ra. Ra, ra, ra.

The Hawk

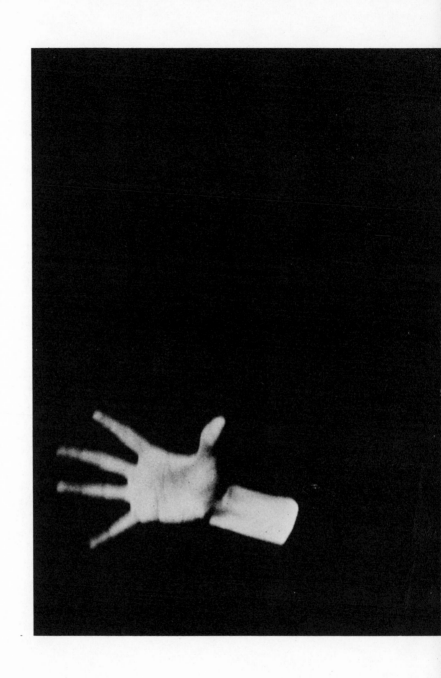

He returns to stage left.

Man fears fire. Ever since he is a kid. His parents would yell: "Stanley! Keep your hands off that fire!" So the kid gets a social prohibition. Yet man has a strong affinity for the fire. The heat resembles the warm blood of the body, the flickering flame is the vitality of life; and the blue flame is the phallic symbol, the smoke is the female sex organ. So man gets a complex between the social prohibition and his fascination for the fire. So he goes to the psychiatrist, or analyst. And the analyst tells him to lie down on the couch, and man talks himself out of walking into the fire.

He returns to center stage and walks into the "fire." As his body writhes and struggles as the burning man, his voice describes the event:

The feet burn, the legs burn, the body burns, the arms burn, the skin blisters and peels, the juices burn up, the arms try to push the fire away, the mind tries to control the body, the flames rise, the throat burns, the nostrils burn, the muscles contract, contract, the hair is burning, the head is burning, the eyes pop out, the eyes pop out, the body contracts, contracts, the head! head! head! the mind can no longer control the body, the body contracts, contracts . . . the body falls to the ground.

He goes to stage right.

The body falls down to the ground, yet the fire keeps on burning, and burning, and burning.

He bows and exits.

.

The Hawk

4

Part I

The Hawk
6

The HAWK *enters.*

Hawk: This is not an ordinary apartment. Junkies come here. I don't take junk myself. I sell it. The size of the apartment . . . well, it starts here *[following the edge of the stage]*, goes to here, and along here, down and across. This is a wall *[stage right]*, it's blue. This is a wall *[upstage]*, it's blue. And this wall *[stage left]* is blue. There is a rug which covers the entire floor. Wall to wall. It's blue. It's a nylon synthetic rug. The reason it's synthetic is that if you spill a drink or throw up on it, I can clean it. A sofa *[the three chairs]*. A blue sofa. A modern, conventional, box type sofa. I sit in it. Sometimes I sit here and sometimes I sit there. The table *[in front of the chairs]*. This is a very practical table, in that sometimes it's here and sometimes it's not here. It has a glass top. That's because when you look through you can see the blue rug. I keep the table clean and clear of all things. *[crosses to upstage left, opens a door]* The bathroom is ordinary. Sink, shower, john, and *[facing rear wall]* . . . What the fuck do you call that? It's . . . a medicine cabinet. *[crosses to upstage right]* The kitchen. Refrigerator, sink, stove, cabinets. All in various shades of blue. I keep a lot of food in the refrigerator. Food I eat and food I don't eat. Junkies don't eat much. *[crosses to downstage right]* The liquor cabinet is lined in blue. I keep it refrigerated. For the champagne. *[crosses to the single chair]* This is a very comfortable chair. It's blue. Velvet. A 1920's-1930's barrel chair. When you sit in it your arms rise up. It's the kind of chair Jean Harlow sat in. Nobody sits in this chair. Nobody ever sits in this chair. *[crosses to* *downstage center]* This is a mirror. It completely covers this entire wall *[the fourth wall]*, from the ceiling to the floor. *[crosses behind the sofa]* Well. Do I have everything? Sofa, chair, bathroom, kitchen, rug, walls, cabinet, mirror . . . I think I'll go out.

He starts to leave. The DOUBLE intercepts him. They open the door together.

Double: Where are you going?

Hawk: I was going out.

The DOUBLE enters, crosses to the single chair and sits. The HAWK closes the door and sits on the sofa. The DOUBLE begins reciting the HAWK'S litany. The HAWK repeats after him, phrase by phrase. As the litany is repeated over and over the HAWK rises and circles the stage. At a point they reverse—the HAWK recites, the DOUBLE repeats. The litany builds to a peak—the HAWK leading, the DOUBLE subsiding. Finally the HAWK stands before the mirror, loudly reciting the litany by himself.

The Hawk
9

The Hawk's Litany

*The hawk. The hawk is an animal. An animal is
hungry. That's why he kills. He kills because he's
hungry. The hawk is hungry. He finds a victim. He
attacks the victim. He kills the victim. He takes the
victim into the sky, back to his nest, and he devours
the victim. Because he's hungry. That why he kills.
Because he's an animal. An animal is hungry. The
hawk is an animal . . .*

The HAWK stops suddenly.
The DOUBLE rises.

Double: Did you score?

Hawk: Yeah. I have everything. The heroin. Morphine.
Pot, coke, orange soda, champagne, tea, food . . . *[sits]*

Double: *[indicating a box]* The box. This is a wooden box.
It's from Tangiers.

Hawk: Veracruz.

Double: Veracruz. It's a hand-carved box and in the center
there's an engraving of a fire god. The fire god has two blue
sapphires for eyes. The inside of the box is lined in blue
velvet and contains a syringe and two needles. The syringe
has two parts . . .

Hawk: The plunger and the receptacle.

Double: The plunger and the receptacle. Of the two
needles, one is long and the other short. One is gold and the
other silver. I'll put these back in the box here and close it.

Hawk: Ornithological.

Double: Yes, this is the most important object in this ornithological tragi-comedy of life and death, love and hate, war and peace.

Hawk: O.K.

Double: [*returns to his chair*] Now, if you ever want this box, if you ever need it, just ask me for it, and I'll give it to you.

Hawk: Now.

    Double: Wait.

      Hawk: Wait.

        Double: Wait.

          Hawk: Wait.

            Double: Wait.

              Hawk: Wait.

                Double: Wait.

                  Hawk: Wait.

                    Double: Wait.

                      Hawk: Wait.

                        Double: Wait.

Hawk: She's coming.

Double: She's coming.

Hawk: She's coming.

Double: Wait.

Hawk: She's coming.

Double: She's coming.

Hawk: Wait.

Double: She's coming.

Hawk: Wait.

Double: She's coming.

Hawk: Wait.

Double: She's coming.

Hawk: She's coming.

Double: Wait.

Hawk: She's coming.

Double: Wait.

Hawk: She's coming. She's coming. She's coming. She's here.

They both turn and look at an empty space in the sofa as if someone were sitting there.

First Improvisation: The Imaginary Victim

Hawk: She's skinny.

Double: But she has a great walk.

Hawk: A sequin dress . . .

Double: . . . in the early darkness . . .

Hawk: And a certain oriental . . .

Double: . . . roll to her . . .

Hawk: . . . hips. She's anything but cherry.

Double: She has the sweet . . .

Hawk: . . . pale . . .

Double: . . . look . . .

Hawk: . . . of the damned.

Double: Just like . . .

Together: Jean Harlow.

Hawk: But she's skinny.

Double: Yeah.

Hawk: She looks hungry.

Double: Maybe you should give her something to eat.

Hawk: Yeah, that's a good idea. *[he feeds her]* There.

Double: She's a fast eater.

Hawk: Scoffs it right up, doesn't she?

Double: You know, not eating is unhealthy, self-destructive.

Hawk: I'll give her some more. *[feeds her]*

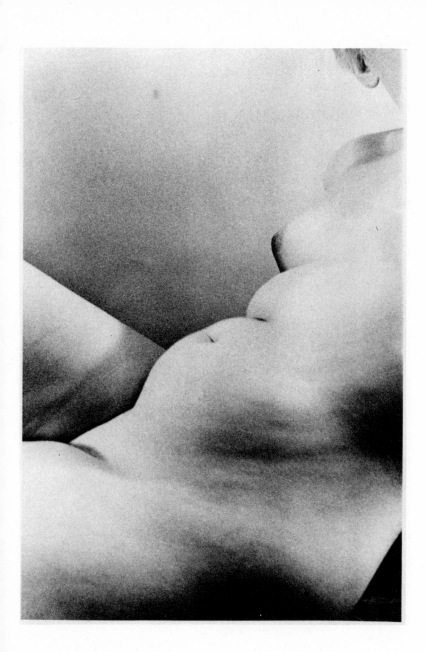

The Hawk
17

Double: Aside from the nutritional value, there's also the simple pleasure of eating.

Hawk: Look, she's filling out.

Double: Sure is. In fact, eating is one of the most important activities that fill our day.

Hawk: She's much healthier looking.

Double: Give her some of that spaghetti there.

Hawk: She Italian? *(feeds her)*

Double: Everybody eats spaghetti. The Chinese invented it.

Hawk: Look at that.

Double: Yeah. Give her some more.

Hawk: *(pries her "mouth" open and stuffs it)* Down it goes.

Double: She's really getting fat now.

Hawk: Yeah.

Double: More.

Hawk: Yeah? Here you go, baby. *(throws it into her)*

Double: Wow. Look at that.

Hawk: *(moving off the sofa to make room)* Fantastic.

Double: Will you look at that flesh!

Hawk: I'm looking at it.

Double: Do you see the flesh on her?

Hawk: It's there all right.

Double: Pink, juicy flesh.

Hawk: Pink, juicy flesh.

They turn and watch her "image" in the mirror.

Hawk: She's huge. Gigantic.

Double: Look at that stomach.

Hawk: Look at that stomach.

Double: Do you see the flesh on that stomach?

Hawk: Look at that stomach.

Double: Look at those arms.

Hawk: They're enormous.

Double: Look at the flesh on those arms.

Hawk: Just hanging there.

Double: Look at those legs.

Hawk: Those legs.

Double: Fat, juicy legs.

Hawk: Oh, legs, legs, big legs.

Double: Look at those breasts. Do you see those breasts? All the meat on those breasts.

Hawk: Mounds of flesh.

Double: Pendulous boobies. Flesh everywhere.

Hawk: Look at it roll! I want her.

Double: Succulent, juicy . . .

Hawk: I want her.

Double: Limitless flesh . . .

Hawk: I want her.

Double: You want her?

Hawk: Yes, I want her.

Double: She's ripe.

Hawk: I want her! I want her!

Double: You can have her.

Hawk: I want that flesh. *(moves to the mirror)* I want it. I want to devour that flesh.

Double: You can have it.

Hawk: I want to rip and tear and bite into every bit of it.

Double: Take it.

Hawk: I want it. I want that flesh. I want it now. Right now. I want it. Yeah! I want it! I want it! Now! Now! Now! *(to DOUBLE)* Now.

(The DOUBLE brings the box. The HAWK prepares an injection and gives it to the "victim." A pause. They watch "her" as she falls to the floor.)

Double: I think she O.D.'d.

Hawk: Easy come, easy go.

The HAWK goes to the bathroom and takes a shower.
The DOUBLE rearranges the materials.
The "VICTIM" lies on the floor.

> **Double:** *(in the kichen, repeating the gestures of the HAWK'S shower)* A kind of anxiety appearing verbiage. Is what it is. He reassures himself. About the real. But there's something . . . signs . . . there are

signs . . . yes, there are signs, signals . . . yes, signals
we give . . . to one another in our passing . . . in order
to create warmth . . . light . . . yes, but we must see
that the light and the dark and the warm and the cold,
the good and the bad . . . the actual pain we suffer . . .
between them . . . that's not right . . . not "between,"
no . . . the actual pain we suffer . . . in the process . . .
the process? Is illusory, not real, is the void . . . therefore, a reflection on the surface of the . . . whatever
. . . a glance . . . the droplets of meaning adding to a
force . . . a power . . . a demon . . . which he confuses
with himself. Verbiage.

The DOUBLE escorts the "victim" out.
The HAWK and the DOUBLE return, as before.

Double: She's dead.
Hawk: She was skinny but she had a great walk. A sequin
dress in the early darkness and a certain oriental roll to her
hips. She was anything but cherry. She had the sweet, pale
look of the damned. Just like Jean Harlow.
Double: What do I do with the body?
Hawk: The body?
Double: Her corpse. She's dead.
Hawk: I turned her on.
Double: They'll be looking for you.
Hawk: What do you expect me to do? I can't help it.
Double: Get rid of the body.
Hawk: I can't.
Double: Get rid of the body.
Hawk: I can't.
Double: Get rid of the body.
Hawk: I can't.
Double: Get rid of the body.
Hawk: I can't. I can't. I can't.

The FIRST VICTIM appears at the door

Second Improvisation: The First Victim

Hawk: *(opening the door)* Yes?

Victim: Hiya. I'm Joanie.

Hawk: Yeah?

Victim: Marilyn Stein's friend?

Hawk: Marilyn . . . oh, come in.

Victim: *(entering)* Oh, thank you. *(sees the mirror)* Oh, my!

Hawk: You're Joanie?

Victim: Uh, yes. You know, that is the biggest mirror I have ever seen. *(they both look in the mirror)*

Hawk: Sit down.

Victim: *(sitting)* Thank you. Ah, Marilyn said that if I ever wanted to reach her, I should come here and maybe you could tell me where I could contact her.

Hawk: Marilyn Stein?

Victim: Yes.

Hawk: She's a friend of yours?

Victim: Oh, my closest and dearest.

Hawk: Wait here. *(goes to the kitchen)*

Victim: My goodness, it's so blue here, and everything matches.

Hawk: *(handing her a "bottle")* Here.

Victim: Oh, thank you . . . Orange soda! My favorite. *(drinks)* Marilyn said you were a very gracious person. Ah, do you know where I could find her?

Hawk: Excuse me. Your name is . . . ?

The Hawk
23

Victim: Joanie.

Hawk: Joanie Stein.

Victim: No, Marilyn Stein. I'm Joanie . . .

Hawk: Oh, yes, you're Marilyn's closest and dearest friend.

Victim: Yes. Joanie. Do you know where I could contact her?

Hawk: Marilyn. Ah, let's see, she was living in this pad downtown, but she had to leave for some reason, and I don't know where she is right now.

Victim: Oh? *(disappointed)* Oh. Well, does she ever call you?

Hawk: Well . . . yes, as a matter of fact . . . That's right, she called me this afternoon. Yes, Marilyn called this afternoon.

Victim: Isn't that something. You know, Fate is just playing with me today.

Hawk: How's that?

Victim: Well, when I arrived at the Port of Authority . . .

Hawk: Where?

Victim: The Port of Authority?

Hawk: Fate.

Victim: I mean, it's funny that Marilyn should call you today. You see, I was thinking that maybe Marilyn would put me up until I could find a place of my own.

Hawk: Where are you from?

Victim: Brooklyn.

Hawk: Did you run away?

Victim: Well, I never thought of it like that . . . I just left.

Hawk: Listen, if you need a place, you can stay here for a couple of days.

Victim: You know, Marilyn told me that you were a very kind and gracious person. I can tell why.

Hawk: Do you want to stay here? It's cool . . .

Victim: Oh, no, I couldn't. Really, it would be too much bother . . .

Hawk: No, not at all. One of us could fall out on the floor and the other could . . .

Victim: What did Marilyn say when she called?

Hawk: Oh . . . she said she would be here about 11 or 12 . . . 1 . . . 2 . . . 3 . . . 4 . . .

Victim: I told you. Didn't I tell you?

Hawk: What?

Victim: Fate.

Hawk: Fate?

Victim: Playing.

Hawk: Right. *(gets up, goes to kitchen, returns)* Have another orange soda.

Victim: That is really very nice of you.

Hawk: You know, I knew this man once who was convinced that his number was up. So he decided to stay in for a week. Then one day he thought he heard someone calling his name. He went to the window, opened it, and looked out. No one in sight. But he kept hearing his name. He leaned out farther, and then turned to look behind him. His wife was standing there, she had been calling to him from the other room. Then it happened—he jumped up, banged his head on the window, the window broke and severed his head at the neck. It was all over in a flash. Fate. How long have you known Marilyn?

Victim: Oh, we grew up together. Ever since we were kids. We went to high school together, and the dances on weekends, and to Dubrow's . . . We even had a whole cha-cha routine worked out. And Bay Two, and Manhattan Beach . . . Did she tell you anything about me?

Hawk: Well, only that you were a close and a dear friend.

Victim: That is so true. You know, she told me an awful lot about you, too.

Hawk: She did?

Victim: Oh, yes. How terrific you were and what a kind and gracious person you were. And what wonderful times she had here and everything like that. And that sometimes when she came, ah, she would sometimes get . . . high?

Hawk: Get high?

Victim: Ah, yes, and she thought that since I was her closest and dearest friend, that maybe I could come here and get high too?

Hawk: You want some grass?

Victim: Not exactly.

Hawk: Pills? I have uppies, downies, Seconal . . .

Victim: Ah . . . heroin?

Hawk: You take heroin?

Victim: Ah, sometimes.

Hawk: I see. Well, sure.

Victim: Oh, I knew it. I could tell. This really is my day.

Hawk: Oh, listen, I should apologize, I haven't offered you anything to eat. Would you like a little something?

Victim: Oh, no, thank you. I couldn't, really. See, when I was at the Port of Authority, I had a frankfurter at the Nedick's they have there. I wasn't really hungry or anything, but my mother said never to go with an empty stomach. And with the excitement of the day . . . ah, do you think I could have my shot now?

Hawk: You look like you should eat more. You look skinny.

Victim: No, I'm just slender . . . if I could just have my shot . . .

Hawk: You know, it's not very healthy to be as thin as you are. You really should make an effort to eat more. I happen to have some food here and I would feel much better if you ate something.

Victim: Oh, I couldn't, really . . .

Hawk: I have some salami, potato chips, frozen pizza, pickled herring, peanut butter; or something more substantial, like pastrami, canned ravioli, Spam . . .

Victim: Really, I just ate. If I could . . .

Hawk: You know, eating is very important. It is one of the most important activities that fill our day. Besides the nutrition it brings, there is also the pleasure it gives. Not to eat is unkind, unhealthy, and self-destructive. Besides, I won't give you the shot unless you eat something first.

Victim: Well, maybe I could force down a bite or two.

Hawk: Good. *(he gets up and brings the food to her)*

Victim: *(eating)* You know, this is very strange, but it really reminds me of a dream I had the other night. I dreamt that I was starving . . . oh, barbecued chicken. My mother always makes boiled. This is my favorite. Mmmmmm. Delicious. As I was saying, in this dream, I was so hungry that I had these terrible pains in my stomach. But I couldn't find anything to eat. And there were all these people around handing me Care packages, only when I opened them up they turned out to be full of garbage! Coffee grounds, rinds, potato peels . . . and then, all of a sudden, I was in my mother's kitchen, and there was my mother at this huge stove cooking chicken soup in a great big pot and I asked her for a kreplach, so she reached into the soup and pulled out a kreplach and she threw it on the floor. I bent down to pick it up, and, what do you think? She stepped on it! "Mother," I said, "could I have another kreplach, please?" and she took out another one and threw it on the floor and when I reached for it she stepped on it again and when she took her foot away, underneath was my sister and the kreplach went into her mouth, so I went right in after it and, what do you think?, I was sucked into my sister's mouth and there I was suspended in this dark room, and all of a sudden the lights came on and I was at a dance where everyone was wearing tunics and eating turkey legs and on the cha-cha they would bite into the turkey legs and on the cha-cha-cha they would throw the bones at me! Then I started running away through a dark corridor that changed into a refrigerator, one of those enormous wholesale meat refrigerators, and there were these huge sides of beef hanging all over, and I knew that, at last, here was my dinner. So I went over to a side of beef and I started eating and eating and eating, and I started to get fat. And I got fatter and fatter until the flesh was hanging from my body layer after layer and I tried to walk but I could only waddle. That's when this small white duck came waddling up to me and as it was waddling it lost its feathers and then it lost its skin and then there was this raw duck waddling beside me as I waddled to the next side of beef and I ate and ate and I got fatter and fatter until the only thing I could move was my mouth. *(pauses, eating)* Then I woke up. Oh, seedless grapes. I thought they were out of season. They're my favorite.

Hawk: Here, have some tomato juice.

Victim: Do you have a piece of lemon?

Hawk: Of course. *(he gets the lemon)*

Victim: This is really so nice of you. I just wish I was a little hungrier. Do you think Marilyn will be here soon?

Hawk: Marilyn? Oh, no, I don't think Marilyn is going to make it tonight. I just remembered, she's a dyke.

Victim: I beg your pardon?

Hawk: I said, "I don't think Marilyn will be here tonight. I just remembered that she's a dyke."

Victim: That's what I thought you said.

Hawk: You see, she has this new lover uptown and she was concerned about your coming here because she knew that if you met this person it would make you unhappy . . .

Victim: I do not comprehend what you are saying.

Hawk: I said that she is making it with this new chick now and she doesn't want to see you.

Victim: This is not a very funny joke.

Hawk: Besides, you can't depend on dykes to come when they say they're going to do.

Victim: Wait a minute. Wait a minute. I cannot sit here as Marilyn's closest and dearest friend and listen to you cast aspersions . . .

Hawk: Oh, come on, she told me about the two of you. Don't play dumb with me. Your lover's making it with someone else. I told you you can't depend on dykes, not for anything. They're just unreliable.

Victim: . . . on my closest and . . . I mean, you've been very gracious up till now and a joke is a joke, but I will not sit here and listen to you go on damaging the character of my closest and dearest . . .

The Hawk

Victim: I'll just have to leave. *(goes to the door)*

Hawk: What about the heroin?

Victim: *(stops)* Do you think I could have my shot now?

Hawk: Sure. You ready?

Victim: Do you think . . . ?

Hawk: Sit down there, on the rug. *(to DOUBLE)* Now. *(the DOUBLE delivers the box and returns to his chair. The HAWK slowly and methodically prepares the injection.)*

Victim: *(sits)* I don't understand why you're saying these things. I mean, Marilyn and I are the closest and dearest friends, and just because two human beings happen to be able to be close and communicate with each other doesn't mean what you said. I mean, if I don't know Marilyn, who else could know her? We're the closest and dearest of friends and you don't find a friend like Marilyn every day of the week. I mean . . . I mean, she was such a good friend to me. She would do anything in the world . . . like the time her Uncle Max invited her up to the bungalow colony and she wanted me to have just as good a time as she did. And that was the best time I ever had . . . Marilyn and I did everything together . . . that's what matters, when two people can care about each other . . . and communicate . . . and do things together. I mean, Marilyn is the best friend I ever had, and, I mean, she's really a good friend, and . . . and I understood . . . I mean, when she started taking heroin . . . I understood . . . and when I was just a little afraid at first . . . I mean, she understood . . . and that's . . . and even when we had this plan about leaving Brooklyn together and she left a little before me . . . I understood. And I'm sure she understands now . . . that's what a friend is. That's what it's all about, not what you said. When two people can talk to each other and understand each other. And be together.

Do everything. You don't find that every day in the week! I mean, Marilyn and I . . . I . . . I mean, I would do anything in the world . . . and she would do anything in the world for me, and that's what is really important. That's what really matters . . . when it's all one . . . when two human beings can care and understand and communicate and be together . . . that's what it's all about! That's what . . . *(he gives her the shot)* . . . really matters . . . what really matters . . . when it's all one . . . *(She starts to get up. A flash. She slumps to the floor, dead.)*

The HAWK *takes another shower.*
The DOUBLE *rearranges the materials.*
The VICTIM *lies on the floor.*

> **Double:** *[in the kitchen, repeating the gestures of the HAWK'S shower]* He is overcome by the abstract gestures of animals. Snouts . . . scurrying . . . feet in the hallway . . . wings knocking . . . Birds fly out of networks of trees, shrieking. Straight down. Heading straight down. Images exploding. "That's where it's at," he says to himself. He grabs a piece and runs. He's still heading straight down. He screams. He doesn't hear himself. Someone is laughing at him. The laughter is slow, hollow. He forces. He claws. He grabs. He dries himself in the sun.

The DOUBLE *escorts the* VICTIM *out.*
The HAWK *and the* DOUBLE *return, as before.*

Double: She's dead.
Hawk: She was skinny but she had a great walk. A sequin dress in the early darkness and a certain oriental roll to her hips. She was anything but cherry. She had the sweet, pale look of the damned. Just like Jean Harlow.
Double: What do I do with the body?
Hawk: The body?

Double: Her corpse. She's dead.
Hawk: I turned her on.
Double: They'll be looking for you.
Hawk: What do you expect me to do? I can't help it.
Double: Get rid of the body.
Hawk: I can't.
Double: Get rid of the body.
Hawk: I can't.
Double: Get rid of the body.
Hawk: I can't. I can't. I can't.

The SECOND VICTIM *appears at the door.*

Third Improvisation: The Second Victim

Victim: *(breezes in wearing a psychedelic outfit, checks herself out in the mirror)* What's happening?

Hawk: I give up.

Victim: Hey, I brought you a present. *(outlining a large box)* It's a big present.

Hawk: Should I open it?

Victim: Yeah.

Hawk: *(opening the "box")* What's in it? *(victim stands in place of the box ... shrugs ... they turn away)*

Hawk: How about a Coke?

Victim: No, that's O.K. I've got one here. *(outlines a Coke)*

Hawk: Have a real one.

Victim: No, I'm getting to like these. Do you want one?

The Hawk

The Hawk
36

(She makes him a "coke". He takes it. She puts hers in a "cabinet" and begins doing a thing with the cabinet, changing it into various objects.)

Hawk: Not bad. You got any root beer in that thing of yours? *(no response)* Just Coke. Coke, Coke, Coke.

Victim: *(stops)* You know, I did the funniest thing the other day. I was just like walking down this street. I'm walking down this street, and I see this fat man. *(outlines the man)* This little fat man. And he looks terrible. Really down. So I say to him, "Que paso, little fat guy?" And he says, "I want to get high." So, I think, if he wants to get high, he should get high. But, like, I don't have any grass on me. So, I say to him, "Come with me, little fat guy." We start walking down the street and he's kind of, like, waddling next to me and we keep walking until we come to this narrow little alley. And at the end of the alley there's this . . . ah . . . door. Yeah, door. *(makes a door)* So, I open the door and I look around and it's very dark. But, it's O.K., because I've got my candle *(makes a candle)*, and I light my candle, and I see . . . two boxes. We sit down on the boxes and the little fat guy says, "I want to get high." Well, I still don't have any grass, right, so I go . . . *(makes a joint and smokes it)* . . . you know how I do . . . and I go *(smoking the joint)*, and I pass it to him, and he smokes it, and I go *(makes another joint, smokes it, passes it)* . . . like that. And we sit there for a while, doing that. Nothing happens. Then, I look over at him, and he's not just a little fat guy anymore, he's a *stoned* little fat guy. I mean, like he's smashed out of his head. I can hardly believe it. That's cool, because it's all an illusion anyway.

Hawk: *(rolling a joint)* Care for a smoke?

Victim: Yeah. *(takes a toke, holds it)* Dynamite. *(another* *toke, looks toward the door)* Was that somebody at the door?

Hawk: No, there's no one at the door. If there was someone at the door, I'd be the first to hear it.

Victim: Well, I don't know. I get paranoid sometimes. And there's a lot of bad shit happening lately. Like, just the other night I was sitting over at a friend's pad. A quiet evening. There was someone in the kitchen doing some stuff, and the rest of us are hanging out in the living room smoking some nice hash. A quiet evening with friends. And I'm just sitting there grooving. And all of a sudden I hear this sound

outside, this kind of tapping sound, like, tap, tap, tap. Well, I can't figure out what's happening, so I open the window and I look out, and what I see, over on the corner, is this cop. And he's standing there with his nightstick *(makes a nightstick)*, just kind of tapping. Then I look down at the other end of the block and there's this other cop and he's tapping with his nightstick, too. Then I look up and down and around and the street is full of cops tapping with their nightsticks. So, while I'm trying to work out whether it's Morse code or something, I hear someone yell "Hey, man, they're coming through the fucking windows!" Then there's this whole scene with people running into the bathroom to

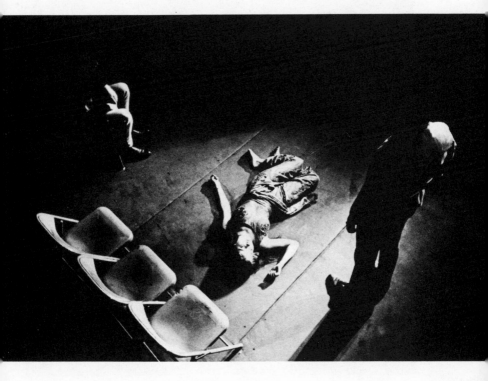

The Hawk

The Hawk
40

flush their lives away, and needles breaking and all like that, and I crawl out on the firescape to see what's happening. And, man, there's cops everywhere, thousands of them, rushing up and down dragging people out into the street and throwing them into wagons. I mean, they don't care who the fuck it is, they're just grabbing people. Like there's this cat just walking down the street, you know, minding his own business, and he gets his head smashed by a cop with a nightstick and there's blood pouring all over the place and across the street this chick is screaming her head off, and there's people smashing bottles and slashing and hitting and kicking and this wild scene, I mean they got bricks and garbage and shotguns and teargas, and there's blood and gore and people screaming and dying *(thrashes about on the floor)* in the gutters and it's horrible and nobody knows what to do. Like, it's blood and people's insides and gore and screaming, wow! *(stops)*

I mean, like, you can tell why someone would get paranoid. *(sits)* Are you sure there's no one at the door? *(goes to the door)* I'd better check.

Hawk: It's cool. Nobody's there.

Victim: Yeah, you're right. There's no one there.

Hawk: Listen, I've got your stuff. Why don't you . . .

Victim: You know what you need?

Hawk: What do I need?

Victim: You need a radar set.

Hawk: Listen, I have to go out . . .

Victim: *(making the radar set)* With that whoosh, whoosh, scanning device, and in your case a camera; yeah, a camera.

Hawk: Look, I'll give you a box and you can take it with you.

Victim: And you put this on the roof, see, and bring down an extension cord and attach it . . . ah . . . here, to this control panel *(outlines a control panel)*, and up there *(the mirror)* you have a huge screen. Now you just sit back and wait . . . when something's happening you'll get a beep, beep, beep thing and . . . there it goes. OK. That means somebody is coming, right? So, switch to the roof . . . ah, do you know those two people? Well, that's all right, they look involved. Zoom to the hallway. No one in the hallway. The stairs. Up the stairs, down the stairs. Oh, and the fantastic thing about this model is that you can get an entire aerial view of New York. Let's see. Switch to aerial . . . wow. Now let's move in closer. To 37th St. and Seventh Avenue . . . oh . . . zoom in on that yellow cab . . . and in the back seat . . . wait a minute . . . do you see that? The taxi-cab driver isn't the same as his picture! This is unbelievable. What you could do with this machine. You could spy anywhere. Rule the world. You can even get this very room. You can see everything that's happening in this fantastic blue room. In the kitchen, the bathroom . . .

(The Hawk makes a tool kit and attempts to dismantle the "set." She maneuvers to avoid him)

The Hawk

The Hawk
43

Victim: Right in this very room. And you can get a close up or move way back and you can get a side view, three quarter, full face. And you can make it bigger than life or *(he has a hammer now)* you can make it smaller than life and you can even make it very, very small, so like nobody can get to it. But, sometimes you want to change the image. Like it's not very cool to have the same image all the time. *(tries to change the "image," continues hammering at the "set.")* I mean, it's a drag, man, you want the image to change, right? You don't want to always have the same image, the same stupid image. *(they both beat the set)* You want to change the image. To . . . change . . . the . . . image . . . wow! Ah, I think I'll take my bag and split, OK?

Hawk: Sure. *(makes a needle and hits her arm)*

Victim: What's that?

Hawk: Junk. *(hits her again)*

Victim: Yeah. Could you give me my junk?

Hawk: Here. *(hits her again)*

Victim: No man, that's nothing. I want some junk. *(he hits her again)* I mean, that's nothing. If that worked, do you think I'd come to you? Look! *(she makes a needle and hits him)* See, that's nothing. *(he hits her)* Wow! *(she hits him)* I just want some junk. *(he hits her, she hits him, they fight with the "needles")* OK. All right. I'll fight for my junk. Here! No, man, that's nothing. Fingers, you dig? I mean, nothing. All right. Yeah. OK. No, that's nothing, nothing. I don't want that. I want junk. OK. *(she makes a huge needle and pushes it into him, he continues hitting her)* No! That's nothing! *(they face the mirror, he pounds at her body)*

The Hawk

44

Victim: That's nothing. I want junk. I mean, what's that? That's nothing, man! No. I want junk. I don't want that, no, junk, I want junk. I don't

Victim: want acid or Demerol, I want junk. I don't want any coke! Junk! Junk!

Hawk: Here, junk. My entire supply: heroin, morphine, Methadrine, Demerol, acid, Seconal, mescaline, DMT, peyote, junk, shit, opium, hash, junk, junk, cocaine,

Hawk: Here, coke, more coke, Coke, coke, Coke!

Hawk: Coke, coke, Coke, coke . . .

Victim: *(heading for the door)* Just give me my bag and I'll split.

Hawk: *(stops)* Sit down on the rug and I'll straighten you here. *(to* DOUBLE) Now.

The DOUBLE *delivers the box and returns to his chair. The* HAWK *prepares the injection.*

Victim: *(sits)* You're a fucking drag. I mean, like it's very hard to make it when people fuck with your thing like that. Like you got your thing and I got mine and you could have the exact same one if you wanted it. Like . . . people . . . like they're really stupid and vicious. Like when somebody just goes and claws out a piece of your thing. And then . . . like, yeah, they start thinking that someone else makes up all the rules for their little games and they think there's some great almighty thing up there that really cares what the fuck they do with their stupid games . . . and who cares . . . like animals . . . yeah, animals know what to do. They got one thing and they go out there and they go after it. But people, they get all hung up . . . with objects . . . yeah, like you don't see a lion stalking through the jungle in search of a double boiler. Or a bird checking his watch. Animals really know . . . and then people, like they put them in zoos. But they don't say, "Dig the groovy animal, he's doing his thing." No, they say, "Look at the funny animal." People get so fucked up, I can't believe it. It's crazy is what it is . . . it's really crazy. It's a whole crazy mess. You got to be crazy to stay here. I mean, like I'm going away. Yeah, I'm going away. But you can't just *(makes a car)* drive to Connecticut or someplace like that . . . you got to *(makes a train)* take a train to the coast . . . or *(makes a boat)* a boat to Tangiers or Ibiza . . . or . . . Oh, no man, I'm going to take a jet *(makes a jet)* . . . yeah, a jet. A big silver jet, with wings and windows, no, no windows, just one big window in front and inside there's this control panel *(makes the panel)*, and I can just get into it . . . because it's my jet, yeah, it's not anybody else's jet. It's all mine. It's all my thing. Like I can get into anything I want to . . . and I can just be up there and a lot of sky and blue and clouds and go anywhere and leave all that pink people babble and just stay up there and go and do anything and be alone *(the* HAWK *gives her the injection)* . . . and not have any stupid games bumping into me . . . and be there . . . and go . . . just go . . . wow *(a flash, she dies)*

The HAWK *takes another shower.*
The DOUBLE *rearranges the materials.*
The VICTIM *lies on the floor.*

> **Double:** *(in the kitchen, repeating the gestures of the* HAWK'S *shower)* There was once a musician who, each night at nine, would blow his horn out the window of his apartment. He was all right. He could get into it. He had a good dramatic sense. He was playing for a chick he dug—she lived in the building

behind his, on the other side of a small cemetery. It was a routine, a serenade. First he fiddled around a bit, announcing his presence, working himself up. When he found a riff he could play with, he got louder and came on with the vibrato. It started to get painful. He must have really had it in for that chick. After a while, he gave up on the music part altogether —the horn yelped and moaned and got all frustrated. Finally, he went into this one, long, screaming high note . . . and fucked it for all he was worth. Which was enough to blow your brains out. I guess he got his nut off, but he was doomed to repeating it . . . each night at nine . . . until she split or he busted his lip . . . or something.

The DOUBLE escorts the VICTIM out.
The HAWK and the DOUBLE return, as before.

Double: She's dead.
Hawk: She was skinny but she had a great walk. A sequin dress in the early darkness and a certain oriental roll to her hips. She was anything but cherry. She had the sweet, pale look of the damned. Just like Jean Harlow.
Double: What do I do with the body?
Hawk: The body?
Double: Her corpse. She's dead.
Hawk: I turned her on.
Double: They'll be looking for you.
Hawk: What do you expect me to do? I can't help it.
Double: Get rid of the body.
Hawk: I can't.
Double: Get rid of the body.
Hawk: I can't.
Double: Get rid of the body.
Hawk: I can't. I can't. I can't.

The INSPECTOR appears at the door.

The Hawk
47

The Hawk

Fourth Improvisation: The Inspector

Inspector: *(enters wearing a trench coat and hat. He flashes a badge in the mirror, inspects the room, then encounters the "body")* The body. *(inspects it)* No pulse . . . incipient rigor . . . dead two and a half hours . . . overdose of heroin. *(rises, begins a reconstruction of the crime)* He is sitting here *(couch)*. He's five feet tall, brown hair, blue eyes, 185 pounds . . . there's a knock at the door. She enters . . . five foot three, 120 pounds, 27 years of age, blue eyes, green feet. She crosses over and sits down. He brings her an orange soda. They begin to talk. Does he know Marilyn Stein? Yes, he knows Marilyn Stein and she . . . *there's a knock at the door.* She comes in. Five foot two, *127 pounds, 17 years of age,* red hair, red eyes, psychedelic jump suit . . . sits down. He hands her a Coke . . . there's a knock at the door. She enters. Five foot three, 185 pounds, 47 years of age, Indo-Eurasian graduation gown . . . crosses over and sits down. He gets up and goes to the bathroom and gets her a cup of tea . . . There's a knock at the door. She comes in, five foot three, blond hair, blue eyes, black dress, 285 pounds . . . crosses over and sits down. He comes back, hands her the orange soda. She drinks the tea. She asks him if he has a headache. "No, I don't have a headache." "Would you like something to eat?" Yes. She goes to the television set, turns it on. He goes into the bathroom, takes six aspirin, comes back out, sits down. She gets up, goes to the kitchen, comes back with six eggs, eats the eggs. He goes into the bathroom and brushes his teeth. Marilyn Stein . . . a possibility. She goes to the champagne, takes a sip of champagne, he steps on her foot, she sits down, looks in the mirror, the mirror collapses on her face, she runs into the bathroom, the medicine cabinet jumps to the floor, closes, opens, slams in her face, she runs into the kitchen, takes the sink, flushes it down the commode, comes out and spits in his face. He goes into the bathroom and returns with a dead baby sandwich. He eats the sandwich. Uh, huh. He turns around in the form of an anopheles mosquito, buzzes about, flips over the couch, lands on a horse, rides into the bathroom, back out dressed in cleats, stands on her face, kicks her, she doesn't like it, jumps over the couch, he takes a lasso, lassoes her hair, drags her into the kitchen and slams her head in the refrigerator door. Oh . . . There's a knock at the door. A car drives in, the chauffeur gets out, opens the door, nine Packer football players come out, run into the bathroom, turn on the radio, take off their clothes, run back out, get in the car and drive off. Marilyn Stein, Jeffrey, Packers . . . possibilities. She's lying on the floor now, doing a hula dance, in a hula skirt, with a hula hoop. Red Ryder is sitting over here, he throws a spear, it gets Little Beaver, who falls on the floor and turns into 47 Mexican bongo players, the bongoes turn into saxphones which turn into 78 exact replicas of Jean Harlow humming Beethoven's 24th Sonata. She gets up, goes to the mirror, the mirror splatters, the room turns blue, he swims toward her in a scuba suit, takes a harpoon and gaffs her ear, her ear turns into a cornucopia. Coins fall out, he picks them up, goes into the kitchen, takes out a frying pan, beats on it, hears the sound of the frying pan, she's beginning to bleed, her heart is throbbing on the floor, he takes a nine iron and chips it into the wall, the room turns red, the iron turns into a snake, coiling into her ear, eating her, digesting her, he goes into the kitchen, takes some Saran Wrap, wraps her head in it, her head leaps from her body, bounces on the floor, bouncing up and down. He leaps in the air, grabs a vine, swings back and forth, dressed as Tarzan, lands over here, where he keeps his stash, starts swinging again, she's lying on the floor, throbbing, begging, pleading . . . yes, that's it, yes, she's here for dope. The kitchen runs into the bathroom, the bathroom into the kitchen, the medicine cabinet jumps back on the wall, the mirror decollapses. He swings over to her, she's here, dressed as Dale Evans, burning up, he grabs a pen wiper, cuts the vine with the pen wiper, grabs her arm, the vein is throbbing, pulsing, he vines her vein with the vine, raises the pen wiper and is about to insert it into her vein . . . Which is where we come in. *(addressing the mirror)* There's really no need for this kind of thing. None at all. We have a situation set up, which is comparable to this only it's under more beneficial, controlled circumstances. He proceeds in this amateuristic fashion, thus convicting himself, I'm afraid. There's no need for it. If he wanted to see us, if he made an effort, if he had something on his mind, some sort of desire, some sort of feeling, some sort of lust, some need, flesh need, hair need, eye need, soul need, mother need, father need, rock, tree, earth, sun, sound, sky need . . . he could have come down and seen us. It's a simple matter. You take the crosstown shuttle. The building's 87 stories high, black, no windows, you can't miss it. This particular crime is very common, *homo sapiensis romantismus phantasmagorias,* RP for short—it's located on the 13th, 22nd, 34th and 88th floors. We have miles and miles of files, prints, charts, graphs, ideograms, caligragrams, telegrams, every conceivable aspect dealing with this particular operation, desire, need, felt emotion, whatever it was, we have it for him. You see, he has something on his mind. Something that he is seeking. We know what he was seeking, don't we? Some sort of fulfillment. What was it? Some supreme emotion? The feeling of his body moving through space, weightless like a bird? We have birds on tape, he could have been a bird. If he wanted to learn Chinese we could have transplanted the head of one of our Chinese people. There's no problem. We could have done this, done it all, for him.

The Hawk
51

That's what we're there for, to help. Help, help, help. But, no, they insist on going about it their own way, you see, and this is where they fall short. Then we're called in. And more's the pity, I'd say. It's bothersome. For me, for us, for everybody involved. And yet, it's so simple. So easy. He could have come in and sat down, given us his name, his number, his need, whatever it was, we have it. We check his print, his chart. We have his cellular development, his genetic background, his father's, mother's, sister's, his son's, heirs' to come, their genetic background, their cellular divisions, the history of his cells, chromosomes, past, present, future, their evolutionary development, on film, as they're developing in his body. Everything that he is, will be, hope to be. Everything that has been. We have all this. We could have done this for him. But, no. No, no, no! He proceeds in his own shoddy, little, amateuristic way. Insisting on his own method, flipping and flopping about. Why did he do this? Why? Why? Why? So simple a matter, so simple a matter. Was it love? Love? Love? Or hate. What? What was it? Images? Sounds? Did he want to hear the sound of a liner meeting the dock? The longshoremen singing at night? We have that. We have World War II on tape. We're working on World War III. What was it? A baby's cry? Hob-nailed boots? We could have given him this! Charts, prints, graphs, files, miles and miles of files! Anything! In perfection! Control! Whatever it is. Come in, give us your number, we have it for you. Anything you want! The world in the palm of your hand! The universe! Equations! Arithmetic! Alice! Method Alice! The birth of a star! A galaxy moving through space! Space moving through a galaxy! What is it? We have it! All of it! We have it! All! . . . controlled . . . *(stops)!* We left him here. Our friend, the bird. He inserts the needle into the vein. The heroin, an overdose, in this case, courses through the vein,

12 seconds of time, into the heart. The victim experiences a flash of joy . . . 13 seconds later, death. He gets up, goes into the bathroom, undresses himself, looks in the mirror and steps into the shower. Well, this concludes the case. Except for the motive . . . the motive. Oh, there's someone in the kitchen. There's someone in the kitchen and he's eating. He's eating. Yes, yes, of course. The motive is hunger. *(leaving, stops)* Odd, she resembles a K109BC . . . a saint. *(exits)*

The DOUBLE *addresses the mirror.*

> **Double:** Yes, I have known a lot of psychopaths—bad amphetamine heads, bad junkies, father haters, killers, hard guys, slow talkers from Texas, droolers, silent tea heads, schizoid dykes, cokeys, racial fanatics, flipped out husbands . . . The one thing they all have in common is a certain freedom of action—they just don't give a shit. They have their thing to get them off, whatever it is, in the head . . . And I should say also, for your information, that drugs do not make psychopaths, psychopaths make drugs, as they make war, as every man is a potential psychopath. . . .

End of Part I

Part II

The Hawk
58

The HAWK and the DOUBLE are as before.

Double: She's dead.
Hawk: She was skinny but she had a great walk. A sequin dress in the early darkness and a certain oriental roll to her hips. She was anything but cherry. She had the sweet, pale look of the damned. Just like Jean Harlow.
Double: What do I do with the body?
Hawk: The body?
Double: Her corpse. She's dead.
Hawk: I turned her on.
Double: They'll be looking for you.
Hawk: What do you expect me to do? I can't help it.
Double: Get rid of the body.
Hawk: I can't.
Double: Get rid of the body.
Hawk: I can't.
Double: Get rid of the body.
Hawk: I can't. I can't. I can't.

The THIRD VICTIM appears at the door.

Fifth Improvisation: The Third Victim

Hawk: Who is it?

Victim: Madame Duval.

Hawk: Who the fuck is Madam Duval? *(opens the door)*

Victim: I am Madame Duval.

Hawk: What can I do for you?

Victim: Well, you must know me.

Hawk: No, I don't.

Victim: Well, you know my chauffeur, Jeffrey.

Hawk: Oh, come in.

Victim: *(enters, looks in mirror)* Oh, what a marvelous mirror. Absolutely charming. *(turns)* You know, I had a terrible time getting here.

Hawk: Oh, really.

Victim: Oh, yes. It was simply awful. It's Jeffrey's night off, you know. I think everyone should have one night off, don't you? It breaks the monotony and refreshes the spirit, in a manner of speaking. Well, where was I? Oh, yes. So I came by taxi instead. Have you ever tried to get a taxi over here? It's really quite an experience. You stand out in the street and shout "Taxi! Taxi!" And, of course, they're all going to Brooklyn. And then there's the ones with their off duty signs on. So, you shout, "Off Duty! Off Duty!" Of course that does no good whatsoever. And when I finally got one, the driver talked incessantly all the way over, about some person named Jackson or Johnson . . . it was simply unbearable.

Hawk: Would you like something to drink?

Victim: Oh, yes, how sweet. *(she talks to her "guides," who hover somewhere over her left shoulder)* What's that, darlings? Oh, yes, the blue . . . you're quite right . . . very poor taste . . .

Hawk: *(at the liquor cabinet)* What would you like? I have champagne, some whiskey, Scotch . . .

Victim: Oh, no—I'm English.

Hawk: No, what would you like to drink?

Victim: I would like tea, please.

Hawk: Tea. How do you take it?

Victim: I take it with one level teaspoon of sugar and a twist of lemon floating in the glass.

The Hawk

The Hawk

Hawk: Certainly. *(goes to the kitchen)*

Victim: *(arranging herself in a rigid position)* Ommmmmm.

Hawk: *(returns with the tea)* Are you all right?

Victim: Oh, yes. I was just composing myself. I feel relaxed now. More relaxed than I was before, which isn't very relaxed, but it is more relaxed than I was before.

Hawk: I see. *(hands her the tea)*

Victim: Oh, thank you. Mmmmm. Delicious. Have you known Jeffrey long?

Hawk: Two, three years.

Victim: He's a dear boy. He's been with me for some time now. His friends, though, they're a bit odd. Bohemians, I suspect. Charles . . . that's my husband, he's the nervous sort, you know, with blue eyes and baggy trousers. Charles thinks that Jeffrey is a common criminal. Hardly. A bit common, perhaps, but certainly not criminal. Wouldn't you say?

Hawk: What can I do for you?

Victim: Oh, yes. Of course. Excuse me . . . what's that, my dears? . . . yes, yes . . . patience, we'll go soon . . .

Hawk: Who are you talking to?

Victim: Oh, that . . . my guides.

Hawk: Your who?

Victim: My guides.

Hawk: Oh, you're one of those . . . ah . . . Christian Scientists?

The Hawk

Victim: Not exactly.

Hawk: They talk back to you?

Victim: We communicate, of course.

Hawk: How many do you have?

Victim: Two. How many do you have?

Hawk: I have one.

Victim: Oh, bully for you.

Hawk: I think one's enough. Any more than that and the room would start to get crowded. Two of anything is more than I can stand. *(pause)* What did you come here for?

Victim: Oh, yes. Well, I was going to call you. On the phone, of course. It's Jeffrey's night off, you know. And I had the receiver in my hand, when they said to me, "Emily" . . . they call me Emily.

Hawk: Is that your name?

Victim: No. "Emily," they said, "go yourself." And I said to them, "But surely I could just call a messenger service and have them deliver it in a plain white wrapper!" But they insisted. "That is not discreet," they said, "go yourself." So, I came myself.

Hawk: Why?

Victim: Oh, yes. I'm so forgetful at times. Well, to get to the point, it's about your merchandise. Yes, your . . . what's that noise? Do you hear that?

Hawk: What noise?

Victim: That flapping noise. It's getting louder. It's coming closer. *(rises, backing away around the room)* . . . it's the beating of wings . . . it's coming closer . . . it's a bird . . . a huge bird . . . it's coming closer . . . it's coming towards me . . . it's a . . . it's a hawk! . . . and it's coming towards me! No! Stop! Stop it! Get away! Get away from me! Stop! Stop! *(pause)* Well. They certainly are playful little devils. Now, what was it you came to see me about?

Hawk: I live here. You came to see me.

Victim: Oh, yes. Quite right. It is rather confusing sometimes. They can throw me off, as it were. But it's much better now. I went to a psychiatrist, you see, and my problem was cured in three months' time. He said I was the fastest client he ever had. Charles sent me. He was upset when I told him I could hear voices. I was upset too, because it got to be very distracting when I couldn't tell whether they were talking to me or just having a little chat with one another. So, I went to the psychiatrist, and after three months, I was able to hear them loud and clear . . . yes, darlings, we're hurrying right along.

Hawk: The merchandise.

Victim: Oh, yes, about the merchandise. How shall I put it? I feel . . . yes, of course . . . we feel that a better brand is the best solution.

Hawk: What do you mean?

Victim: Well, I mean that whatever you have been giving us has been . . . I hate to use the word inferior . . . but inferior it has definitely been.

Hawk: It's not working.

Victim: Well, it does produce a mild nausea and splitting headaches, but these aren't exactly the effects we had in mind. So, we thought that if you could prescribe a better brand, we would be most appreciative.

The Hawk
65

Hawk: How long have you been taking morphine?

Victim: Oh, let's see . . . I've been taking syrettes now . . . thank you, darlings . . . eighteen months.

Hawk: I see. Well, what you have is very common among junkies. You've developed a tolerance for the drug. Most addicts suffer from this. It's very common.

Victim: Ah, yes, junkies, poor sufferers.

Hawk: You need more. Six syrettes instead of three.

Victim: That wouldn't be very practical, would it?

Hawk: Practical?

Victim: Well, of course, with such a busy schedule, people coming to see me for guidance and readings . . . and there's Jeffrey . . . why, that would mean he would be at my side morning, noon, and night . . . hmmmm.

Hawk: Later on, you'll probably need nine. But, I assure you, it happens every day. As long as the cost doesn't bother you, you needn't worry about it. Most junkies are poor.

Victim: Yes, of course. Well, I hardly think it necessary to dwell on that. Besides, if your theory had been correct, they would have said to me, "Emily, you need more injections." Now, wouldn't they?

Hawk: It makes no difference to me. You'll need the six injections sooner or later. Your body just won't stand it. That's the reason for the nausea and the headaches. Now, do you want . . .

Victim: Excuse me . . . what's that, darlings? . . . oh? Oh, really . . . well . . . (to HAWK) "Emily, you need more injections." That's what they said. Now, if you have a sterilized needle, some alcohol, and gauze, we can put your theory to the test.

Hawk: You want to try it now?

Victim: Oh, yes, by all means.

Hawk: How do you take it?

Victim: One level teaspoon of sugar and a twist . . .

Hawk: No, the injection. Where do you take the injection?

Victim: Well, I used to take it in the arm, but I found that when I appeared before a multitude—sometimes it's more like a minitude—to speak, and I raised my arms, well, the marks weren't exactly in keeping with the spiritual nature of the occasion. So, I take it in the ankle, alternating one here, then one here. I find that to be most efficacious. Although, I can't remember which ankle was last . . . Jeffrey sees to all that, of course.

Hawk: How about if I give it to you up your ass?

Victim: Well, if you think . . . up my what?

Hawk: Jeff was saying to me the other day how the old junkie likes it up her ass.

Victim: *(goes to the door)* Could you open this door? Could you please open this door?

Hawk: *(opens the door)* I'll send Jeffrey over with the usual amount.

Victim: *(leaving)* Yes, that would be just fine. *(turns)* The usual amount! Oh, really! Do you mean to say that I've come all the way over here, stood in the street waving for a taxi, sat in this horrid blue room drinking luke warm tea, chased by that abominable hawk, to have you say to me, "Up my ass!" Well, up your ass! The usual amount, indeed.

The Hawk
67

Hawk: See that worn spot on the rug?

Victim: Yes.

Hawk: Sit on it. All of you. I'll give you the shot. *(to DOUBLE)* Now.

The DOUBLE delivers the box and returns to his chair. The HAWK prepares the injection.

Victim: *(sits)* Well . . . yes, in a minute, darlings . . . we must endure . . . a junkie, indeed . . . sit on the floor . . . isn't that just too, too bohemian . . . it's not as though we haven't sat on floors before. We have sat on floors . . . sometimes we were fortunate enough to sit on mattresses . . . choking from incense . . . little boxes with colors on them . . . it's all so common . . . how they manage, I don't know . . . they're barely able to communicate with each other, let alone on some higher plane . . . poor Jeffrey. If only he wasn't so . . . well, he is . . . yes, yes, darlings . . . be patient . . . And Charles' friends, oh they're really impossible too. They look at one another and they talk. You can hardly tell them apart, except one is long and one is short . . . I often wonder if they hear each other . . . Imagine Charles worrying about my voices . . . Charles has never heard a thing in his life . . . Yes, yes, my dears, soon . . . A junkie. Imagine, a junkie. Why, for thousands of years civilized man has used stimulants to elevate and communicate . . . to reach the world of the spirit. A junkie! Everyone knows that a junkie is someone who falls, shakes, sweats, has fits and strangles people in dark alleys . . . a junkie . . . Please hurry! . . . Oh, it's so impossible. All of them. Jeffrey's friends. Charles' friends . . . but, I have made efforts. Yes, I have. I have gone out to people and I have said to them, "friend." Yes, I have. And have they extended their hand in friendship? No, they have not. They have hid in their horrid little voids . . . you are the only ones . . . I can speak to you . . . I can communicate with you . . . we talk . . . yes, we do . . . where are you? . . . I say, where are you? . . . *(to HAWK)* Are you ready? Are you ready? *(to guides)* Well, where are you? One joke is enough. Where are you? *(to HAWK)* Please hurry! *(The HAWK starts to give her the injection in the arm)* No, no, in the ankle. Yes. *(he gives her the injection)* There. Now, where are you? Please, darlings . . . *(to HAWK)* I told you! It is not enough! Get more! Get more! *(he goes for more)* Are you there? Are you there? What's that? *(looks in the mirror. A vision seems to come to her)* Of course . . . *(falls to the floor, dead:)*

The HAWK *returns with the other shot. He pauses a moment, then pounds it into her ass.*
The HAWK *takes another shower.*
The DOUBLE *rearranges the materials.*
The VICTIM *lies on the floor.*

> **Double:** *(in the kitchen, repeating the gestures of the HAWK'S shower)* You know, I have moments. I walk around a lot. I go for strolls in the park. I hang out. I observe, sometimes, when my head gets loose . . . when the habitual hairyness . . . subsides . . . I watch them, you, us, the others . . . carry on . . . I have moments. I see the picture. I wonder at this creature I see, who is so far out of the muck, who has shed his gills, who swims for relaxation, who shits into plastic bowls, who searches for love, love . . . I wonder about this need for love, this irrational yearning . . . a torment, in fact . . . especially when you consider what he's made of, what he smells like, what he's capable of doing . . . I wonder if it's built in . . . how deep it runs . . . if it is in the sea! If it is in the sky! In the eyes of cats! Then I get a feeling in my gut just like hunger, a feeling that washes over my balls and up into my lungs, and my heart, and my

The Hawk

brain . . . a useless compassion . . . making me into a dumbfounded idiot! Which disgusts me!

The DOUBLE escorts the VICTIM out.
The HAWK and the DOUBLE return as before.

Double: She's dead.
Hawk: She was skinny but she had a great walk. A sequin dress in the early darkness and a certain oriental roll to her hips. She was anything but cherry. She had the sweet, pale look of the damned. Just like Jean Harlow.
Double: What do I do with the body?
Hawk: The body?
Double: Her corpse. She's dead.
Hawk: I turned her on.
Double: They'll be looking for you.
Hawk: What do you expect me to do? I can't help it.
Double: Get rid of the body.
Hawk: I can't.
Double: Get rid of the body.
Hawk: I can't.
Double: Get rid of the body.
Hawk: I can't. I can't. I can't.

The FOURTH VICTIM appears at the door.

Sixth Improvisation: The Fourth Victim

Hawk: *(opening the door)* Oh, fuck! *(shuts the door in the face of the FOURTH VICTIM, a striking platinum blonde reminiscent of Hollywood in the early 1930's, who opens the door, enters, and crosses in front of the mirror, holds her breast, and poses. She turns.)*

Victim: Hello, fuck-face. *(sits on the couch next to the HAWK)* Hey, Charlie, you like this? *(she presents a perfumed arm under his nose)* It's called Ben Hur. Give it a chance to sink in. A gift from an admirer.

Hawk: Something else. Let's have another smell.

Victim: So, how's your ass, Charlie?

Hawk: It's all right. How's yours?

Victim: I wish you hadn't asked me that. I'm in bad shape, Charlie. I have this huge bruise on my hip. *(hands on hip, outlining a bruise)* You wouldn't believe it. It's not even black and blue. It's all yellow and purple, and there's some green here. And there's this pain that goes down my leg, past my knee *(hands on knee)*, then shoots up the other side, where there's this big scratch across my stomach. I couldn't begin to tell you how that all happened. Oh, and my toe, right on the end, a large sore, and *(presents an ankle)* do you see that?

Hawk: Is that a rash?

Victim: No, cigarette burns. Could you believe it?

Hawk: That's a rash.

Victim: Cigarette burns. I ought to know. I was there. And then there's this piece of bone. Give me your hand. *(his hand on her hip)* I think it's come off and into my . . . yeah, right there.

The Hawk

Hawk: That's a cyst, not a bone.

Victim: No, that's a piece of bone, Charlie, it's a chip. Don't try and scare me. You see my neck?

Hawk: Hickies.

Victim: Look at that. And I have a sore throat, and my back is killing me, my tongue hurts, my tits are swollen . . . *(pause)* Jesus, I got to change my life, Charlie. *(poses in the mirror as she would on a magazine cover)* You know, I've been thinking, just because I'm five feet three and a little chesty doesn't mean I couldn't be a fashion model, does it, Charlie?

Hawk: You want to be a fashion model?

Victim: Well, I have very high cheekbones and long eyelashes and all you have to do is look dumb. I've been looking through a lot of magazines and I could do that. What have you got to drink, Charlie?

Hawk: There's some champagne, help yourself.

Victim: Champagne? What's the occasion?

Hawk: I just thought you might like it.

Victim: You're a real friend, Charlie. *(pops the cork)* Oooooh. *(pours a glass, hand on breast, and swills it down)* So, anyway, this is what I thought: sooner or later people are going to get tired of all these women that are built like boards, you know. They're going to want to see some flesh, right? That's where I come in. I mean, what's a woman without flesh? So, I figure I could just change it all. Can't you just see it? I could become famous. My picture on billboards, TV, magazines all over the country . . . my face. People would start imitating the way I wear my hair and the way I make up. And I could meet someone who would

love me for what I am . . . what movie did I see that in?
(pours another, drinks it) Seen any good movies lately,
Charlie?

Hawk: Yeah, I saw this movie about a hooker who gets
syphilis and dies.

Victim: What the fuck kind of movie is that?

Hawk: Four star.

Victim: You know, Charlie, you wouldn't know a good
movie if it hit you right in the kisser. If you saw *Red Dust,*
you'd be just as stupid afterwards.

Hawk: *Red Dust?*

Victim: Yeah. With Jean Harlow and Clark Gable. It wouldn't change you one bit.

Hawk: I didn't see that movie.

Victim: It looks it. But, don't see it on television. It's not the same thing. You got to see it on the big screen. There's this great scene at the end. *(swings over and throws her arms around him)* She's sitting on his lap and she's got her arms around him.

Hawk: Whose lap?

Victim: Clark Gable. Jean Harlow has her arms . . .

Hawk: Yeah.

Victim: And he's looking down into her eyes.

Hawk: Right.

Victim: And she's looking up into his eyes.

Hawk: Yeah. Then what?

Victim: They have this moment, this long moment, looking into each other's eyes . . .

Hawk: So then what happened?

Victim: I went home. What do you do when a movie ends? *(more champagne)* You probably eat the popcorn left in the aisles.

Hawk: Listen, don't drink too much champagne.

Victim: Oh, I won't.

Hawk: The other night you threw up all over the floor.

Victim: I didn't throw up all over the floor. I never throw up, Charlie.

Hawk: I have photographs of you throwing up all over the floor.

Victim: Photographs! What kind of pervert are you that takes photographs of people throwing up? You're sick, Charlie.

Hawk: Just watch the champagne.

Victim: *(staring into glass)* I'm watching it. *(drinks it)* Now you watch it. *(pours another)*

Hawk: Put your beak to that worn spot over there and smell it.

Victim: Charlie! They ought to lock you up. You're sick. You know, they ought to put you away behind bars.

Hawk: Hey, listen, why don't you take your shit now and leave.

Victim: Did you ever see *Hold Your Man?* That was with Jean Harlow. She went to prison in that movie.

Hawk: Oh, yeah.

Victim: For a crime that she didn't commit, because Clark Gable, who plays a real rat, kills this guy and he leaves Jean Harlow holding the rap.

Hawk: Yeah, I saw it.

Victim: And he runs away . . . you saw it!

Hawk: I saw it, yeah.

Victim: So she gets blamed for the crime and she's in prison.

Hawk: And she's in this cell . . .

Victim: That's right, wearing a grey uniform, with a peter pan collar . . .

Hawk: And there's this psychopath in the next cell. And he's really got it in for Harlow. So, he pulls apart the bars and he takes a long knife and starts stabbing at her breasts, and then he gives her one in the stomach ...

Victim: She's carrying Clark Gable's baby, only she's not going to tell him, because she's too proud. She wants him to come back on his own. So she waits and waits and she thinks a lot and then she starts to pray. And she prays a lot. And finally, she gets ... what do you call it?

Hawk: Syphilis.

Victim: Religious! You're some kinda mono ... what do you call it, Charlie? You have a diseased mind.

Hawk: She spends a lot of time in the chapel, remember? The prison chapel.

Victim: Yeah, the little room with light shining down. And she prays and prays. Her hair was like a white halo ...

Hawk: Then this chaplain comes in. But he's not really a chaplain. He's an ex-Nazi lieutenant who's posing as a chaplain. And he goes up to Harlow and he says "Kneel down, my child, and I'll bless you." So she kneels down and he ... *(takes "Harlow's head" and pulls it between his legs)*

Victim: Blesses her. "You keep having faith, my child, and don't ever give up what you believe in, because what you believe in is what you are and you can only lose by not believing and if you keep believing in it, you'll get what you want."

Hawk: And she believes that?

Victim: Yes. And she says, "I will, Father, I will." And she kisses his ring ...

Hawk: He's the Pope?

Victim: Well, I don't remember. Maybe that was another movie. Anyway, one day while she's waiting in her cell what happens? That big fat woman, you know, the dyke with the big keys hanging down . . .

Hawk: Barry Fitzgerald.

Victim: I don't remember who played the part. But she comes around and knocks on the cell and she says "There's a visitor to see you." And Jean Harlow jumps up and runs down the hall and pushes open this big door, and who's standing in the middle of the room?

Hawk: The psychopath. Only this time she's not getting away. He takes the knife and starts hacking her to pieces . . .

Victim: Clark Gable is standing in the middle of the room, looking away. He's ashamed.

Hawk: He's ripping at her, slashing at her body . . .

Victim: He's such a rat. But she puts her arms out . . .

Hawk: He cuts off the arms, throws them over his shoulder . . .

Victim: Because she's got a big heart . . .

Hawk: Cuts out the heart . . .

Victim: And she forgives him with her eyes . . .

Hawk: Gouges out her eyes, slices her head off . . .

Victim: . . . And then she runs across the room and throws herself into his arms. *(lands in his lap, arms around his neck)* And she looks up at him for a long time, and he looks down at her for a long time, and they look deep into each other's eyes for a long time, and they have this moment, this long moment *(caresses him)* . . .

Hawk: What the fuck are you doing?

Victim: *(rising)* What's with you? You're a dumb fuck, Charlie. You don't even know a moment when it's sitting in your lap. *(to champagne)*

Hawk: Listen, I have to go out, why don't you take your shit now and leave?

Victim: *(drinking)* I'll think twice before I tell you my favorite movies again, Charlie. I'll think twice. I really feel sorry for you, though. I don't hate you, Charlie, you're too stupid. But I'll think twice. *(staring into mirror)* Charlie, what's the matter with this mirror?

Hawk: What's wrong with it?

Victim: It makes me look like death warmed over. Maybe it's the blue; no, the mirror. Christ, Charlie, I look like a corpse. A corpse at twenty-six. Can you imagine that? She was only twenty-six.

Hawk: What movie was that?

Victim: *Saratoga.*

Hawk: *Saratoga?*

Victim: That's right. Suddenly, right in the middle of the filming, she just couldn't go on. Then she died. At the height of her career. You could see how pale she was. They had to get someone else to finish her scenes. God, it was awful.

Hawk: Sounds bad.

Victim: Oh, it was. Here you are and suddenly, in the next minute, you're gone. It's really horrible. But, that's just a small part of it, you know, Charlie? I mean, sure, they buried her, but she's not dead, not really dead. And that's the difference. She's forever.

Hawk: She's what? Forever?

Victim: You could never understand. It's an idea, Charlie. It's more than . . . what you could understand. It's way beyond you, Charlie.

Hawk: Try me. What's this "forever"?

Victim: Well, like, she'll always be there, somewhere, there, up there . . . white and divine . . . there's more to it than just a body . . . it's a kind of forever . . . that's all, a forever.

The Hawk

Hawk: Wait a minute. I think I got it. Let's see. She's forever, because, no matter what, there will always be Jean Harlow, somewhere. A movie, a photograph, a line in a magazine, a thought of Harlow, she'll be there. That's what makes her forever.

Victim: Yeah, that's right.

Hawk: O.K. Now, picture this. You die. They put you in a box, right? And they lower you into the ground, and throw dirt over you, you're dead, right? Dead. And the worms eat your marrow. Are you going to be forever?

Victim: One thing I hate is a smart ass. *(staggering to champagne)* You know, Charlie, you're depressing the shit out of me. I think I'll brighten myself up a bit. *(pours a glass, looks into it, drinks it)* Liquid diamonds. *(pours another)*

Hawk: Excuse me. *(gets up, heads for bathroom)*

Victim: Where are you going?

Hawk: *(gesturing obscenely)* To piss.

Victim: *(hand on breast, swilling it down, staring into mirror)* Divine! *(pours another, backs up, staring into mirror)* Dinner at Eight was without a doubt the best film I ever made. *(waving her arm)* Whooops! *(spills her drink)* Nylon rug. He can clean it up. *(pours another)* The most important people at M.G.M. supported me in that film. John and Lionel. Marie Dressler. She was a real good friend, Marie Dressler. But Billie Burke, what a dumb cunt she was. Wallace Beery played my husband. He was a rotten son-of-a-bitch to work with. He was. And . . . oooh, that long white dress. Up there, on the top of the stairs in that long, white, satin dress . . . with that slob next to me. Well, you got to make some compromises in this business. But I was beautiful. White . . . satin . . .

Hawk: *(coming out of bathroom)* What's going on?

Victim: Oh, hello fuck-face.

Hawk: You're drunk.

Victim: It's a party, Charlie. We're having a party. What a party, too. Everybody is here, Charlie. When we give a party, it's a party. Ah, what's wrong, Charlie, you look so grim. You don't know anyone. You feel out of place. Too much class. *(he turns)* Oh, don't leave, Charlie. You're a friend of mine, and a friend of mine is special, Charlie.

The Hawk

83

(falls into him, he grabs hold of her) John Barrymore! *(moves away)* Look at him—peeing on the curtain! What a lush! And Marion Davies, she's with Charlie again. You know, he's got the biggest Jingjang in Hollywood. Hey Charlie, *(falls on him, he grabs)* you can stay. You can be Tyrone Power or Wallace Reid. *(moves away)* And here comes Lionel Barrymore, that poor, crippled old motherfucker. And Mack Sennett, and Lupe Velez, and Mary Miles Minter. She's through, washed up, ruined by scandal. It's a hard world, Charlie. Clara Bow is here and she brought the entire team with her. Oh, it's going to be a party, Charlie. *(throws herself on him, he grabs)* Loosen up, Charlie, you can be Fatty Arbuckle, we got lots of coke in the ice box.

Hawk: How about Paul Bern?

Victim: *(moving away)* Oh, the life of the party . . . look . . . there's Ethel Waters, she doesn't get to go to these parties often. How you doing, Charlie? Roll out de wardemelon. *(he moves over to her, grabs her)* What are you doing, Charlie? Cut it out. *(moves away, he follows and grabs her)* Hey Charlie, shape up, you'll never get invited again. *(moves away, he grabs)* Cut it out! I said. What do you think I am—a piece of meat? Charlie! You prick! Get your hands off me! *(he grabs, holding on)* Off! I said, off! You motherfucker! Are you deaf? Get them off, you cunt! You prick! You cocksucker! Off! Get your fucking hands off my body! Off! Off! Off! GET YOUR FUCKING HANDS OFF MY BODY! *(he lets go, she poses, divinely, in the mirror)* Wheeeew! *(he grabs her breast)* Wha . . . ! Charlie, get it off! Get your shitty hand off my breast, you prick! GET IT OFF! CHARLIE, GET YOUR HAND OFF MY BREAST! *(he does, she turns to the door)* I'm leaving. Do you hear? I'm going. Leaving. Charlie? I'm leaving.

Hawk: *(to DOUBLE)* Now. *(the DOUBLE brings the box)*

The Hawk
85

Victim: I'm not coming back, Charlie. I'm leaving for good.

Hawk: How would you like a little taste of shit to pick you up? You look frazzled.

Victim: *(turns)* You're an animal, Charlie. A sick, diseased, perverted . . .

Hawk: Sit on the floor. Don't fall—sit.

Victim: *(returns to the center)* The scary thing is if you're around sick people like that, you begin to feel like it's going to rub off. That's a scary thing. I don't want any of that crap rubbing off on me. I take good care of myself. It's not easy. It's not easy with all this shit around. You have to be careful . . . I shouldn't spend too much time with you, Charlie. You're sick. You're depraved. You can't treat flesh like that, like it's a piece of flesh . . . it's not that. It's not the same . . . There's so much of it around. One diseased pervert after another . . . it starts to rub off . . . I can feel it crawling all over me . . . black hairs and warts and pimples . . . you got to stay clean, you got to take care of yourself . . . it's not the same. It's different. You can't treat it like that . . . it just multiplies. You open the door, and the flesh, the hairs and warts and the stink, it floods in. Through the windows, out of the toilet and the ice box, jumping from the mirror, oozing, hanging . . . flesh . . . I can't open my mouth . . . it oozes inside me . . . into my eyes . . . it comes in through my eyes . . . covering me . . . drowning me . . . it's everywhere . . . flesh . . . but it's not just flesh . . . it's not! . . . it's not the same . . . and I'm afraid to lie back . . . just lie back . . . but I can shut myself, my mouth, my eyes . . . and it can't touch me . . . on the ceiling, where it can't touch me. And I can stay there . . . where's it's white . . . on the ceiling where it's white . . . I can lie back and shut myself . . . No, I don't want to lie there . . . no, I don't want to lay down. It's not a bed. It's not . . . it's white. A white dress. I know what it is. A long white dress. And it's not the same . . . it's a chair. A blue velvet chair. I'm wearing a white satin dress with white feathers, and my hair is white and my face is white and I'm sitting up there . . . in a blue velvet chair . . . it's me and I'm sitting there and I can't be touched, because it's not the same as flesh . . . it's different . . . it's white. It's all white. It's beautiful. I'm beautiful, I'm white and forever . . . my hair, my skin . . . are forever . . . and my face is white. It's beautiful. It's forever. My face is forever. It's always there. It's me. It's me. And that's always, always there. *(the HAWK gives her the injection)* That's me. I'm there. I'm there. Forever. Up . . . there . . . that's for . . . ulp! (covers her mouth, then braces herself on the floor.) Blaaaaa! *(She stares at it, then falls face down in the puke, dead)*

The HAWK *takes another shower.*
The DOUBLE *rearranges the materials.*
The VICTIM *lies on the floor.*

> **Double:** *(repeating the gestures of the HAWK's shower)* Nothing will grow on a dead planet.
>
> I needed the bread. It's over now. It's a picture. Put a frame around it. He did it, the he did it. A memory. Don't bug yourself. Go on. He needed the bread. I felt guilty, but I wanted her. Something had to give. He cuts his off or I cut mine off, or . . . I loved, he hated. There were two of us. No, more. I have to live. He did what he had to do. He was under stress. That's how it goes. Put a frame around it.
>
> Suddenly his life is a movie and he is the hero. The film is absolute. It goes from birth to death. Without a witness, he does not exist. . . .

The Hawk
87

The Hawk
88

I have something to sell. The reason I have something to sell, is the people who want to buy. Or is it the other way around?

Nothing will grow on a dead planet.

The DOUBLE *escorts the* VICTIM *out.*
The HAWK *and the* DOUBLE *return as before.*

Double: She's dead.
Hawk: She was skinny but she had a great walk. A sequin dress in the early darkness and a certain oriental roll to her hips. She was anything but cherry. She had the sweet pale look of the damned. Just like Jean Harlow.
Double: What do I do with the body?
Hawk: The body?
Double: Her corpse. She's dead.
Hawk: I turned her on.
Double: They'll be looking for you.
Hawk: What do you expect me to do? I can't help it.
Double: Get rid of the body.
Hawk: I can't.
Double: Get rid of the body.
Hawk: I can't.
Double: Get rid of the body.
Hawk: I can't. I can't. I can't.

The DEALER *appears at the door.*

Seventh Improvisation: The Dealer

Dealer: *(Enters. He is the same person as the INSPECTOR, except that he wears sunglasses, a vest and a black rain-coat. His hand is held up in front of the mirror as though it contained a small package. He sits on the sofa, waits, then begins a brief reenactment of the scenes, playing all the parts)* Oh, yeah . . . Mmmmmm. Aaaarrrghh! *(coughs)* . . . *(places the package down)* . . . Marilyn Stein? Well, let's see if I can place her . . . I'm Joanie, her closest and dearest friend and I just came from the Port of Authority / Oh, that's cool. The Port of Authority. Well, let's see. She comes by here from time to time / Well, she said, that, I should come to see you if I ever needed anything / Oh, did she? Well, she speaks highly of you too / And I had a funny dream that I turned into a kreplach / Oh, yeah, did you? Well, how about something to eat / Hey, I've got a present for you. It's a big present. Here / Oh, what a surprise. Oh! I'm surprised / And I thought that since I was her closest and dearest friend / Yes, of course. Well, sit right down and have an orange soda and some cantaloupe . . . Oh, sorry I didn't see you come in / Madam Duval. My chauffeur sent me. You know, Jeffrey. Of course. Dear boy, I gave him the day off / You did. Well, that's certainly very kind of you. Ah, how about something to eat? / Gracious, certainly not. I'll just do an Omm chant here on the rug and I'll be perfectly refreshed. Oooooommmmmmmm-bbaaaaaaAAAA! / You know Charlie, I'm so goddamn beat. My tits are sore. My legs are swollen. I've got ring worm of the navel and my whatchamacallit . . . Charlie, you wouldn't believe it. Christ, Charlie, I've got to change my life / And I thought that because Marilyn and I were such closest and dearest friends and because I'm coming all the way from Brooklyn / Well, you just suck that orange pop while I turn down this television / You know what

The Hawk

you need. You need a radar set. Hey. Oh boy, you can make it small and put it on the roof / Well, ah, certainly a home is not a home without a radar set. Bleep, bleep, bleep / What's that? Do you hear that? That flapping sound. Oh, god. There. It's a Hawk. And it's coming for me. It's coming for me and it's biting me. It's biting and chewing and tearing me. Oh, god. It's tearing my flesh off / Oh, it's awful, awful, just goddamn bloody awful. Aaacchhh! / Such a thing I never heard. Just because I'm Marilyn's closest and dearest friend doesn't mean that you can be such a schmuck and call to my face, her, a dyke / Well, you know that's just some people's way of love / Hey, oh boy, I brought you a present / I see I'll have to acquire a taste for presents. What is it? / Oh, boy. It's an illusion. Oh, boy / Oh, yeah, just what I need. Ah, can I get you something to eat? Pizza? Pig pudding? I think we have some chitlins in the back / You know, maybe I should do something that has some social security. Like a meter maid or something like that. What do you think, Charlie / It's a possibility. Now where did she go? Oh / What? What, darlings? No, no, it's all right. They're my guides. Guides—uh! Guides—uh! / I see, well maybe I'd better check on that roast pork / Could I have my shot now / Yeah, we're getting to it. Let's see now you're . . . / blood and guts and gore and smash and crash and pow and wowie screaming and dying, oh boy / Charlie, I saw this movie the other night with Ruth Roman and Gina Lollobrigida. They played two guys who were in love with each other and then there's this great scene at the end when they have this long moment together / Junk! I want junk! What's that? That's nothing. I want junk / Well let's see I have a sofa and a chair and a medicine cabinet and a mirror / Dyke schmike, you schmuck. My closest and dearest . . . Give to me the dope boobie / Now wait a minute girls / Up my ass! Up my ass! A Junky. A Junky! Oh, oh, oh. Oh, my god, we must endure / If you think that I'm going to stand here while you insult to my face my closest and dearest friend a dyke. I am just going to have to leave / Now let's not be hasty / Charlie, I think you got your hands all over my body, Charlie, and I want to be white and divine and forever, so get your mother fucking hands off me / Why yes, certainly / Coke, coke, coke. What's that? I want a present, oh boy / Here I think I have an illusion in this box. If you'll just be patient / I won't. I won't. My guides won't.

The Hawk

Jeffrey won't. My ass won't. No. None of us won't Charlie your hands are so rough and scaly, Christ, Charlie, you're tearing my titty off / I'm leaving. I'm walking out that door and I'm never coming back. I'm walking out. I'm going down that street, down to the nearest movie house and suck popcorn and never coming back. Do you hear that, Charlie? / Hey, I want some junk, oh boy / I'm leaving. Leaving. Open this door, I say. I say, you colonial mother fucker, open this door / Charlie, you're a dumb fuck. I never puke, I never piss, I'm going to be forever, but before I do, I'm leaving you, Charlie. Leaving / Hey, oh boy, hey, I'm going to split. You're such a fucking drag, oh boy / To my face a dyke. Sprrratzzz! Fuck you, boobie, I'm going back to Brooklyn / Wait a minute girls. Now just hold on there. Let's settle down. Now, girls, let's just pile in here. Yeah, right here. Now. Ah, where's that imported box. Ah, let's just make one here, because we're getting ready for it. That's ready for the Now. Are all you girls settled in there? You ready for it? / I'm ready. I'm ready. I'm ready. I'm ready / Yeah, you're ready. OK.

The DEALER rises, raising his hand in the air as if it held a hypodermic syringe.

Dealer: The Now. This is the Now. The Now is what it's all about. This is the Now right here. *(raises his hand, pause)* That was the Now. *(pause)* Dreams, Death and Orgasm. That's now. Bibble, babble, blip, blap bullshit now. That's now. Dreams, Death, Orgasm. Now. That's it right now. That's the Now. *(hand, pause)* And don't you forget it. Dreams, Death and Orgasm is the Now. There's always the Now. No matter where you are you're going to find the Now. Now, you're in the Now. You're dreaming right now. Dreaming now is in the Now. Right? You have an orgasm in your dream. That's a Now in your dream. An Orgastic

Dream Now. And you're dying, that's now. You die, now. You're dead. That's now. *(hand, pause)* AND DON'T YOU FORGET IT. NOW! Now, now, nownownownowNOW-NOWNOW! D.O.D., now. D.O.D. O.D. ODD D.D.O. Now. Do, do, di, now. Do, do, di, oh now. O.D.D. Di, di, do, do, oh, oh D.O.D. That's now. OK. You got Dreams over here. Orgasm here and Death here. Mix them around shuffle them up. Now what do you got here? Where'd you go, Orgasm? Get out of there. Hey, there's Death jumping up and down. That's now. What are you doing Dreams? Dreams is taking a left hand turn on the Now. Swings around and lays a right cross into Orgasm. Smack! OH! Now Orgasm is coming around disguised as a Plymouth Fury. Hard top convertible, white wall tires. A Plymouth Fury Coming around. And here comes Dreams. A pig. Four hundred and fifty five thousand tons of pig is Dreams, baby. A four hundred fifty five thousand ton ham hock pig. And Orgasm is a Plymouth Fury. And over here we got Death. Death will be played in this particular instance as Mickey Mouse. Now Mickey Mouse is a little old son of a bitch with a great big ole long tail and looks like he needs something to eat. Maybe a piece of cheese or a piece of ham. But, don't forget Dreams is ham. Four hundred and fifty five thousand tons of ham. There's a Plymouth Fury. And Mousey's over here. Mousy Death. Mouse ass Death. Mouse eyed, mouse Death. Mouse eye ball Death. Right? OK. Dreams over here. Four hundred and fifty five thousand tons of pig fat now. Next to it is Orgasm. Plymouth Fury, red, hard topped convertible. White wall side tires. One spare coming out the trunk. Driven by nineteen nuns wearing steel rimmed shades. Death is Mickey Mouse. Fuck, no! It ain't Mickey Mouse. It's Mickey Mouse's foot. One inch tall and it talks way up here like Butterfly McQueen and says, "Has it started? Has it started?" And this is the Now *(hand)*. And don't forget it, mother hunches. The Now! Pig ton dreams flopping in. Plymouth Fury coming up fast. Mickey Mouse foot—clip, clop, clip, clop. He's got his thing, you see. It's a foot race. To be qualified to be in this race you had to have a foot. And we caught that cat in the Now. That's how he got that foot. That's where Death came from. He got his foot trapped in the Now. That's Mickey Mouse's foot,—the Now of Death. Coming in solid is Dreams, four hundred fifty five thousand tons of pig puking fat. And over here is orgasm. Plymouth Fury. That's a Now, mother fucker. Moving up fast. Dreams. Death. Orgasm. On the outside come foot. Clip, clop, splat! On top of Dreams. Pig puking Dreams all laid out. Orgasm coming over to the end zone and through the goal posts to score. For the Now. You got to score for the Now. That's now. They're coming in fast. Orgasm takes a left turn. Dreams pops into Orgasm. Uhhhh! Orgasm scoots Dreams in the neck. Eeeekkkkk! Neck turns ear ball Death. Death screams. "Get off my foot!" Neck says, "That simple motherfucker's a seven toed sloth." Splits. And here comes Orgasm moving up fast. Takes a sharp left turn. Pokes Dreams in the eye. Dreams blows her horn. Nineteen nuns do a tuck and roll, knock Orgasm back three paces. Back to Go, baby. Death swings a hard right, bounces off Dreams, does a flip flop, half pike back dive, grabs Orgasm by the ear, pulls nine pounds of pig fat off and throws it in that lady's face sitting right over there. Sorry, madam, but that's life. And that's the Now. Coming up here fast, now. Over here's the Now. Getting closer to the finish line. It looks like . . . Oh, here comes that Plymouth Fury. Foot flop flip flapping over there. Ham hock pig puke coming in. To the Now. Coming up fast. Coming in close. Here they are. Say it, motherfucker. You pick up on that. That's the Now!

The DEALER *returns to where he left the "Victims."*

The Hawk

The Hawk
97

Dealer: Well, let's see, now. As I recall . . . yes . . . *(kneels on the floor)* . . . the, ah, first to go here . . . I don't know why a girl and a girl can't get together. Marilyn Stein was my closest and closest and closest and . . . uhhh! *(hits his arm with the "Now" hand)* . . . OOIII! *(dies)* . . . Number one. Number two is—"Death of a Teeny Bopper" . . . I wanna be up there, Charlie . . . no, that's the other one . . . oh, boy, oh boy, oh boy. A big silver jet. A big silver jet all my own, oh boy. Hey, oh boy, I read the news today, oh boy . . . whaam! *(hits again)* Eeeennnaa / Bogies on the right / nnaaaaaawwwwSplat! *(dies)* . . . Now, let me see . . . that was . . . oh, yes . . . what's that, Darlings? Please hurry. Do hurry along. Yes, darlings? What's that? Up my ass. No. Never. Not while the sun is still never setting . . . what? What darlings? Yes, loud and clear. Ten-four? Oh shit! *(hits again, dies)* Three. And now . . . I wanna be up there, Charlie. Up there. So pure and white and white and divine and forever. Up there. Just me. White and divine and . . . come on, Charlie, fill it up. High octane, Charlie, that's it, pump it in. Yeah. Forever and forever and for . . . ulp. *(hand to mouth)* Ulp! Ulp! Ulp! Blaaaaaah! Blaa! Blaa! Blaa! Blaah! *(pause, then rises)* Yeah. Well . . . oh. *(hands the "box" to the DOUBLE)* I, ah, think she O.D.'d . . . hmmm . . . *(coughs)* . . . ah . . . *(waves to HAWK)* wha's happening, Hawk.

The DEALER goes to the shower and without undressing, steps in and sings this song:

> O, when them poppy balls get rotten
> You can't pick that poppy cotton
> And there's one man can fix you when
> you're down.
> Oh, when them little ole poppy balls get
> rotten

The Hawk

> You can't pick-a very much poppy
>   cotton
> There's that little ole junk man
>   coming round . . . yes, there he
>   is, coming round there, he's the
>   man, oh yes, indeed, oooooh!

The DEALER *leaves the shower, goes to the kitchen, slides palms with the HAWK on the way, takes something out of the refrigerator and eats.*

Dealer: Hmmmm. Delicious. Food's the Now, hey, baby? *(leaving, stops)* Oh, I brought you thirty decks. *(points to the table)* Better watch that stuff—it'll kill you. *(exits)*

The HAWK *and the* DOUBLE *return as before.*
The DOUBLE *begins to speak. The* HAWK *repeats him, phrase by phrase to the end. As the speech builds, the* DOUBLE'S *cool begins to crack as the* HAWK *moves in on his thing. Toward the conclusion, he relaxes again, though bitter and disgusted.*

> **Double:** Considering this mad scramble in its appropriate light, that is, with the correct distance, in focus, detached, we are reduced to the image of a slaughter house on a crust of dirt . . . the crust spins, the sun heats it, the rains cool it . . . the creatures multiply . . . they take it seriously . . . they're at each other's throats . . . they fight for scraps . . . millions are wiped out. Still, they multipy . . . they read the papers, they keep one eye on their neighbors, they copulate . . . there's too many of them . . . there's always too many of them . . . it's an endless supply . . . there's no shortage . . . it fills its quota . . . taking care of business . . . they seem gleeful about it—they jump up and down, they wave flags, they fly in the air,

The Hawk
101

they shout . . . but it's all right . . . it's fertilizer . . .

I am not interested in a solution to my . . . problem. My problem no longer admits to a solution . . . I have become my problem . . . which is the same as having no problem . . . that's right . . . I believe in myself, to put it another way, just like the doctor, lawyer, housewife, and chicken-shit inspector, who will kill, as you know, in defense of their . . . beliefs.

He hallucinates rivals . . . His pleasures are threatened by others. Nameless others clouding his joy. He can't think straight. His eyes burn from the inside out. His fingers peel an endless grape. His laughter is strange, coming at pauses in the conversation. He breaks doors. At night he rolls over into his own skull. His left eye twitches. He's grey before his time. He thinks he's something!

How can I avoid obsessions? Obsessions are criminal. Criminal! The work that I have to do! The work! That is what is important!

WITH WHICH TO TORMENT MYSELF!

What? Aha! Then who is the perpetrator of this . . . OBSESSION? One sees infinity in all directions— that's right. Where does this image come from, that won't let go, this OBSESSION? Why, it arises in the self, that's right, which is a bottomless pit, where there is no one, nothing, to be apprehended . . . for the crime . . .

A kind of anxiety appeasing verbiage. Is what it is. He reassures himself. About the real. But there's something . . . signs . . . there are signs . . . yes, there

The Hawk

are signs, signals, yes signals we give . . . to one another in our passing . . . in order to create warmth . . . light. . . . Yes, but we must see that the light and the dark and the warm and the cold, the good and the bad . . . the actual pain we suffer . . . in the process . . . the process? Are illusory, not real, are the void . . . therefore, a reflection on the surface of the— whatever . . . a glance . . . yet he behaves . . . the droplets of meaning adding to a force, a power, a demon . . . which he confuses with himself. Verbiage! NOW! *(brings the box)*

Hawk: *(preparing an injection with the 30 decks left by the DEALER)* Wait.

Double: Wait.

Hawk: Wait.

Double: Wait.

Hawk: Wait.

Double: Wait.

Hawk: Wait.

Double: Wait.

Hawk: Wait.

Double: Wait.

Hawk: NOW!

The HAWK plunges the needle into the DOUBLE'S chest. The DOUBLE, arms and legs spread akimbo, staggers to the mirror, spins, staggers back, around the room, back and forth, stops, sways, staggers around the room, into the mirror, back, spins, staggers, backwards, stops, sways, goes

The Hawk
107

rapidly around the room, stops, goes back, around, stops, sways, staggers, staggers, sways, stops, sways, now swaying over the worn spot in the rug, sways, sways, suddenly spins about one, two, three times, spinning, falls to the floor—a short series of spasms, convulsions—dead.

The HAWK takes a quick shower, goes to the refrigerator, eats something, puts it back, goes to the DOUBLE and escorts him out.

The HAWK returns as before.

Hawk: The Hawk. The Hawk is an . . . an animal. The Hawk is an animal and an animal . . . an animal is hungry. That's why he . . . he . . . he kills. He kills . . . he kills . . . be . . . cause he's hungry. *(pause)* Because he's hungry . . . that's why he kills . . . he's hungry . . . he takes . . . takes the . . . finds a victim . . . finds a victim *(rises)* . . . attacks the victim. He kills . . . kills the victim . . . Takes the victim . . . *(pause)* . . . he's a Hawk. A Hawk is hungry. An animal is hungry. That's why he . . . kills . . . kills the victim . . . *(circling the room)* . . . Takes the victim into the sky . . . the sky . . . sky . . . back . . . back . . . to his nest . . . and . . . and . . . and he devours the victim. He devours the victim . . . because he's hungry. That's why he kills . . . because he's a Hawk . . . He's a Hawk . . . he finds a victim . . . *(moving into the mirror)* . . . Kills the victim. Takes the victim back to his nest and devours the victim. Because he's an animal. Because he's hungry. That's why he kills. Because he's a Hawk. A Hawk. He's a Hawk. A Hawk. A Hawk! A HAWK! HAWK! HAWK! HAWK! HAWK! HE'S A HAWK! *(pause)* I think I'll go out. *(exits)*

End

THE KEYSTONE COMPANY
Standing from left to right:
Scarlett Johnson
Tony Serchio
O - Lan Johnson
Walter Hadler
Barbara Young
Ching Yeh
Sally Sommer
Lee Kissman
Kneeling:
Tony Barsha
Eddie Hicks
Murray Mednick

The title Keystone is derived from
two sources, the Keystone Dairy Farm,
which we rent and work out on,
and the Keystone comedies of
Mack Sennett.